For Dad, who imagined a marvelous monkey messing with time.

OSCAR ELIOT

ISBN:9781622010172

Copyright 2013 by Oscar Eliot
Published by

www.dcpressbooks.org

this helmet is happy ...

this helmet is happy ...

building!

this helmet is

happy ...

this helmet is happy ...

this helmet is happy ...

this helmet is happy ...

this helmet is happy ...

putting out fires!

this helmet is happy . . .

this helmet is happy ...

this helmet is happy ...

sleeping!

Find your favorite helmet

www.dcpressbooks.org

www.ingramcontent.com/pod-product-compliance
Lightning Source LLC
Chambersburg PA
CBHW040024050426
42452CB00002B/128